Great Lakes Good Times

Summer Vacation Keepsake Book

Crystal
River
Press

Traverse City, Michigan

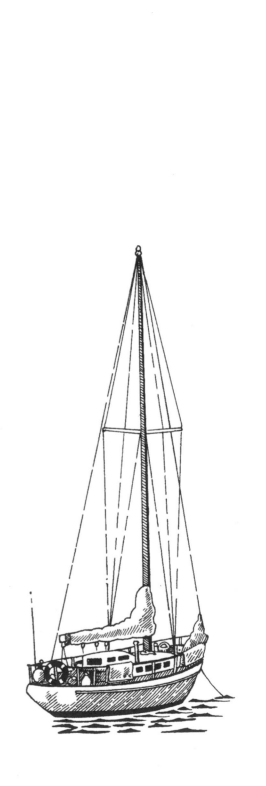

Copyright © 1998 by Mark Dressler
Illustrations by Kristin Hurlin
Book design by Eric Norton

Published by Crystal River Press
135 East Tenth Street
Traverse City, Michigan 49684

Publisher's Cataloging-in-Publication Data
Dressler, Mark.
     Great lakes good times: summer vacation keepsake book /
     Mark Dressler – Traverse City, Mich.:
     Crystal River Press, 1998.
          p. ill. cm.

     ISBN 0-9663578-0-9
     1. Recreation – leisure. 2. Vacation – summer, Great Lakes.
     3. Great Lakes – summer vacation.   I Title.
LCCN 98-65115   1998

Text development by Anne Stanton

02 01 00 99 ❀ 5 4 3 2 1

Printed in Canada

Contents

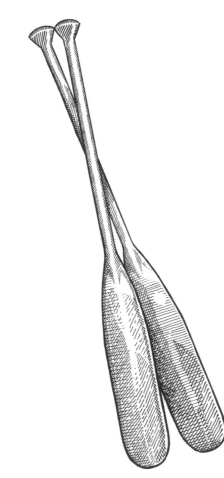

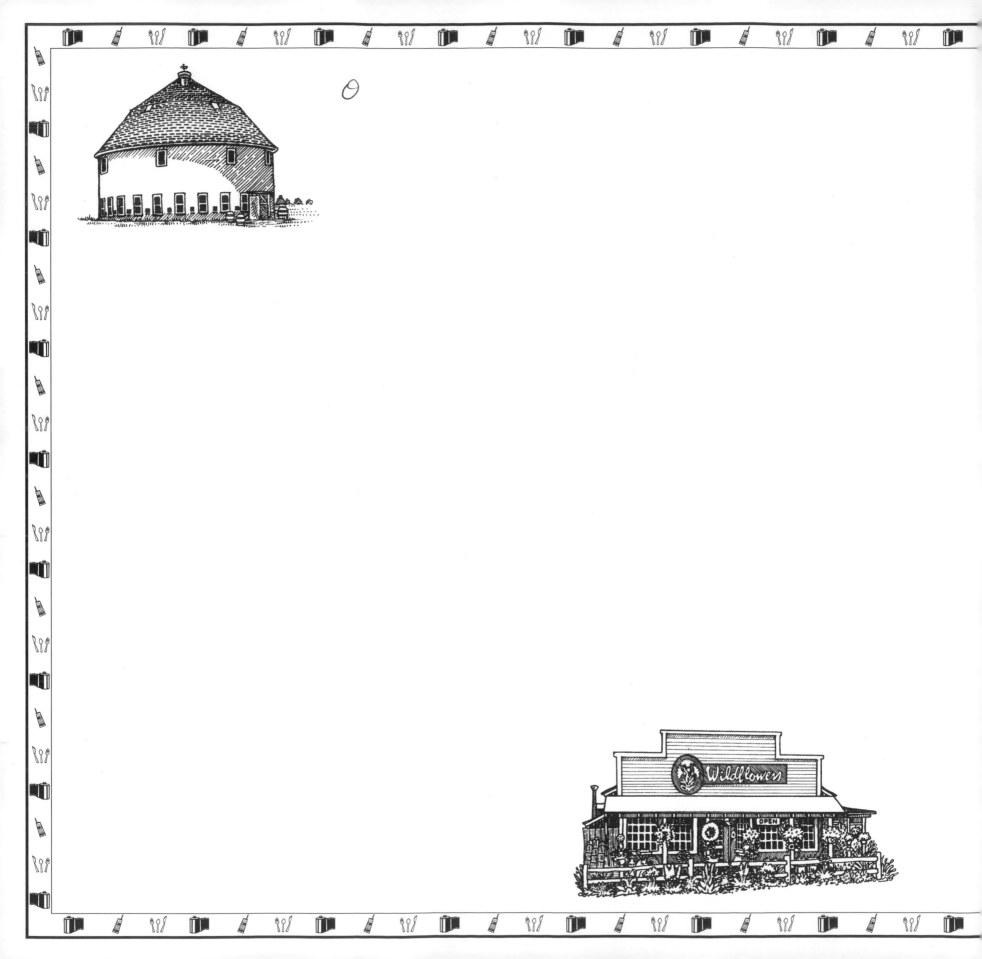

Unique Discoveries

A trip, a safari, an exploration, is an entity different from all other journeys. It has a personality, temperament, individuality, uniqueness. A journey is a person in itself; no two are alike. And all plans, safeguards, policing, and coercion are fruitless.
 – John D. Voelker, late author of *Anatomy of a Murder, Trout Madness* and former Michigan Supreme Court Judge

Unforgettable finds_____
_____
_____
_____

Must-stops. . . . antique stores, farm markets, fruit stands, bed and breakfasts_____
_____
_____
_____
_____
_____

New experiences . . . . saddling up, river rafting,
polka dancing, fishing from a float tube, picking wild blueberries _____
_____
_____
_____
_____
_____
_____
_____

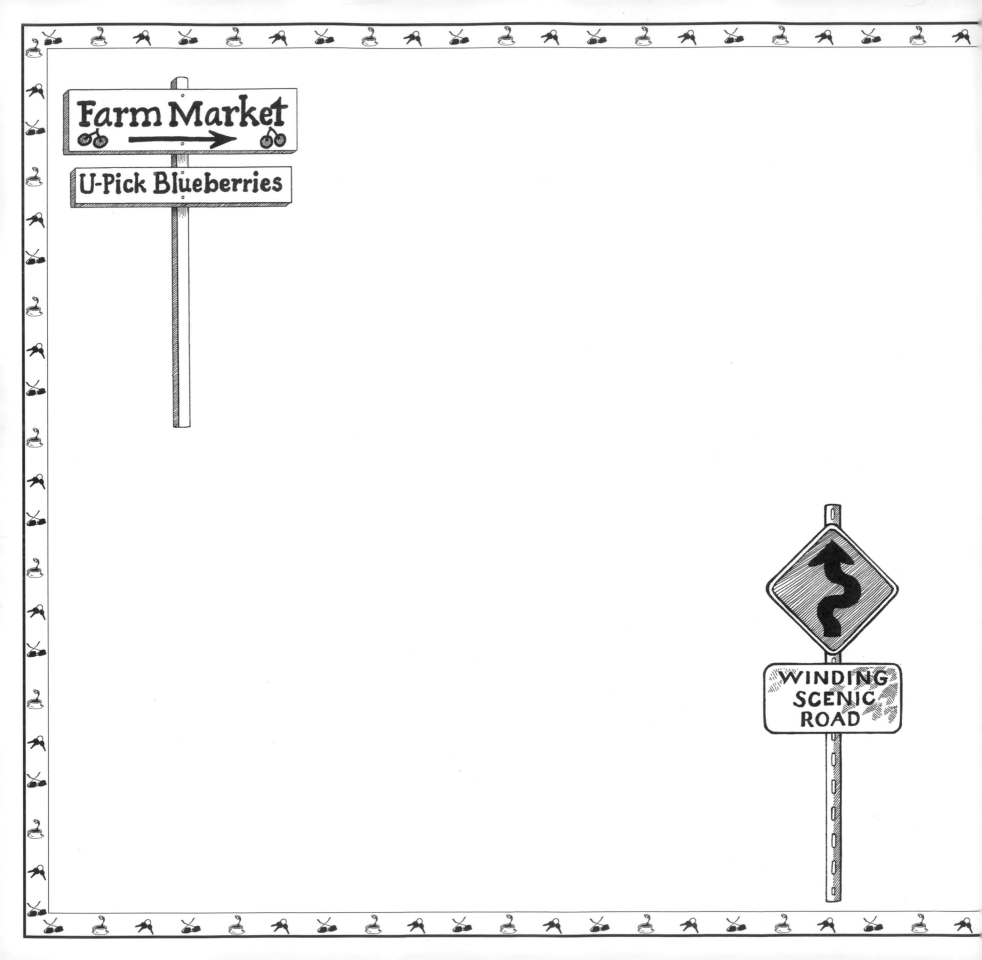

On the Road

We are in a new four-wheel drive which is clearly the ultimate touring car for road comfort coupled with rough-country accessibility. It is packed tight with camping equipment and emergency gear, including an espresso machine that works off the cigarette lighter.

– Jim Harrison, *Don't Fence Me In* from his non-fiction collection, *Just Before Dark*

Our touring vehicle _____

_____

_____

_____

Road trip reflections _____

_____

_____

_____

Our road trip style . . . solo driving,
shared driving . . . hell-bent on getting there,
leisurely stops at every scenic site _____

_____

_____

_____

_____

Peddle power . . . record driving day _____

_____

_____

_____

_____

At the Water's Edge

In no conventional sense are these lakes...They are something else, something separate and unique and wonderful.
– William Ashworth, *The Late, Great Lakes*

Sizzling sands . . . hottest beach spots _____
_____
_____

We waded, swam, sunned, strolled, snorkeled, built sand castles, played volleyball _____
_____
_____
_____
_____
_____
_____
_____

Discoveries . . . driftwood, petoskey stones, rocks, shells _____
_____
_____
_____
_____

Beachside picnics _____
_____
_____
_____
_____

Local Flavor

Anyone who has ever walked around a small village at suppertime on a spring night and heard the sounds of children playing in the park and the choir practicing in the church and watched the mist rising from the lake and heard the redwing blackbirds calling to their mates will know what I mean when I say there is something about village life that calls out to one . . .
– Kathleen Stocking, *Letters from the Leelanau*

Fresh finds . . . basil, sprigs of tarragon, just-picked strawberries, luscious black cherries, fistfuls of wild flowers _____

_____

_____

_____

We've never seen anything quite like this _____

_____

_____

_____

_____

_____

Local characters, small-town traditions _____

_____

_____

_____

_____

Sunrises, Sunsets

I'll tell you how the Sun rose–
A Ribbon at a time–
The Steeples swam in Amethyst–
The news, like Squirrels ran–
  – Emily Dickinson, Harvard Reference No. 318, excerpted

Glorious sunrises _____

_____

_____

_____

_____

_____

Magnificent sunsets_____

_____

_____

_____

_____

_____

_____

Clouds, colors, balmy breezes _____

_____

_____

_____

Joining us . . seagulls, jumping fish,
deer at twilight, fishermen, sailors, kayakers_____

_____

_____

_____

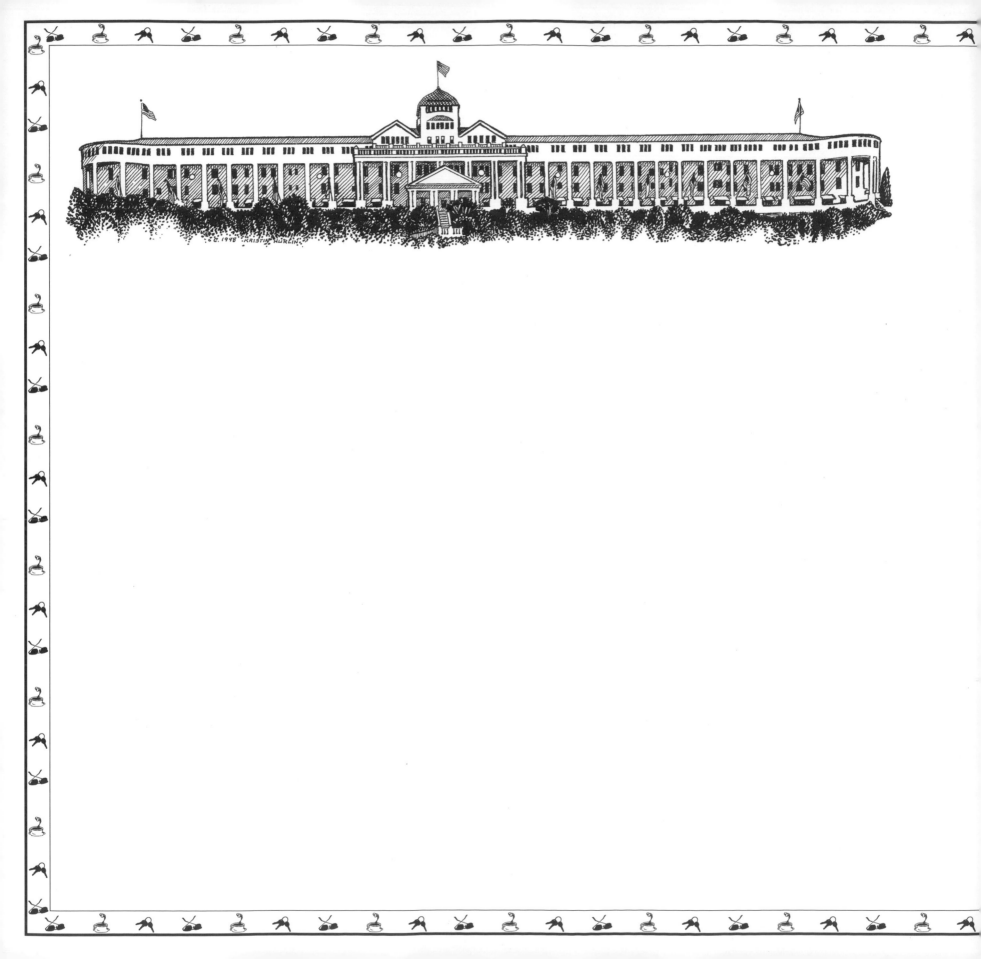

Where We Stayed

The best way to enjoy a trip to these wooded lakes is by camping upon the border of them. . . . You can take your wife and daughter, for a lady in ordinary health could make all the trips outlined above. . . . Awaking in your tent in the morning, you feel like springing up and doing something at once. The resinous air from the balsams and pines heals the irritated glands, dries up the tubercles, and causes even the consumptive to gain a new lease on life.
– A.A. Mosher, *The Wisconsin Lakes* (1890)

On easy street . . . motels, hotels, beautiful B&Bs _____

_____

_____

_____

_____

Camping . . . from primitive to pampered _____

_____

_____

_____

_____

Specialties of the house . . . pool, homemade meals,
lakeside views _____

_____

_____

_____

New Friends

We are not here to see through one another. We are here to see one another through.
– Carol Matthau, *Among the Porcupines*

Unforgettable friends _____

_____

How we met, where we met, things we did_____

_____

_____

_____

_____

Great conversations, stories we shared _____

_____

_____

_____

_____

Addresses to remember_____

_____

_____

_____

_____

_____

Lighthouses

For the lakes are rich in capes, islands, and dangerous channels, beautiful as a dream of blue water and lustrous green isles wooded to their edges—but treacherous by night; and the light-keepers of the Great Lakes deserve a volume to themselves.
– Louise Morgan Sill, *Through Inland Seas, Harper's Monthly,* April 1904

Lighthouses we visited _____

_____

_____

_____

Stories of storms and shipwrecks _____

_____

_____

_____

_____

_____

_____

Landscape, architecture, history _____

_____

_____

_____

Museums, tours, life-saving stations _____

_____

_____

_____

_____

Exploring Our Past

I am in a country where all is life and animation, where I hear on every side the sound of exultation, where everyone speaks of the past with triumph, the present with delight, the future with growing confidence and anticipation. Is not this a community in which one may rejoice to live?

– Anonymous Great Lakes farmer, ca. 1830, drawn from *Michigan in Quotes,* selected and edited by Tom Powers

Preserving memories . . . museums, forts, landmarks, historical sites _____

_____

_____

_____

Pieces of the past . . . antiques, souvenirs, books, old photos _____

_____

_____

_____

_____

_____

_____

_____

Favorite stories of historic buildings, small-town lore, heroes _____

_____

_____

_____

_____

_____

_____

_____

_____

Wilderness Trails

Today I have grown taller from walking with the trees.
– James Russell Lowell

We hiked . . . . . hills, beaches, meadows, pine forests, dunes _____
_____
_____
_____

Animals that crossed our path _____
_____
_____
_____
_____
_____
_____

We walked in . . . . . sunshine, rain, storms, balmy winds _____
_____
_____
_____

Memorable sights and sounds _____
_____
_____
_____
_____

EXPLORE THE WORLD FAMOUS

MYSTERY ? SPOT

Tourist Traps...We Fell Into

Hey, Mom and Dad, look at that cool place with the huge, green dinosaur. Please, please, can't we stop, please, pleeeeeaaassse?
– Anonymous child's pleas overheard last summer

Tourist traps that snared us _____

_____

_____

_____

_____

_____

_____

Our kids actually loved it/will never beg to go there again _____

_____

_____

_____

_____

_____

_____

Our most expensive entrapment _____

_____

_____

_____

_____

CATCH YOUR DINNER
TROUT FISHING
AT THE
GRAYLING FISH HATCHERY

FISH NOW - KEPT FROZEN - PICK UP LATER

By Blowing Hell Trout Farm

NO LICENSE REQUIRED TACKLE and BAIT FURNISHED

35¢ PER INCH

KEEP WHAT YOU CATCH

ICE AND COOLERS for SALE

FISH CLEANING FREE

Off the Beaten Path

We live in a wonderful world that is full of beauty, charm, and adventure. There is no end to the adventures that we can have if only we seek them with our eyes open.
– Jawaharlal Nehru

Ready, get set, explore! . . . Unexpected adventures _____

_____

_____

_____

_____

_____

_____

Magical moments_____

_____

_____

_____

_____

_____

Hidden corners_____

_____

_____

_____

_____

_____

Rivers and Waterfalls

Waterfalls are the flowers of geology. They are showy, extravagant, the liquid equivalent of morning glories in bloom and peacocks in full strut. They are majestic in the way that sunsets, mountains, thunderstorms, and redwoods are majestic, and majesty of that sort has a way of pulling us out of ourselves and humbling us and motivating us to travel hundreds of miles to stand as close to them as possible.
– Jerry Dennis, *The Bird in the Waterfall*

Wild, wondrous waterfalls _____

_____

_____

Untamed rivers _____

_____

_____

_____

_____

_____

Running the river . . . canoeing, floating, kayaking _____

_____

_____

_____

_____

Out for trout_____

_____

_____

_____

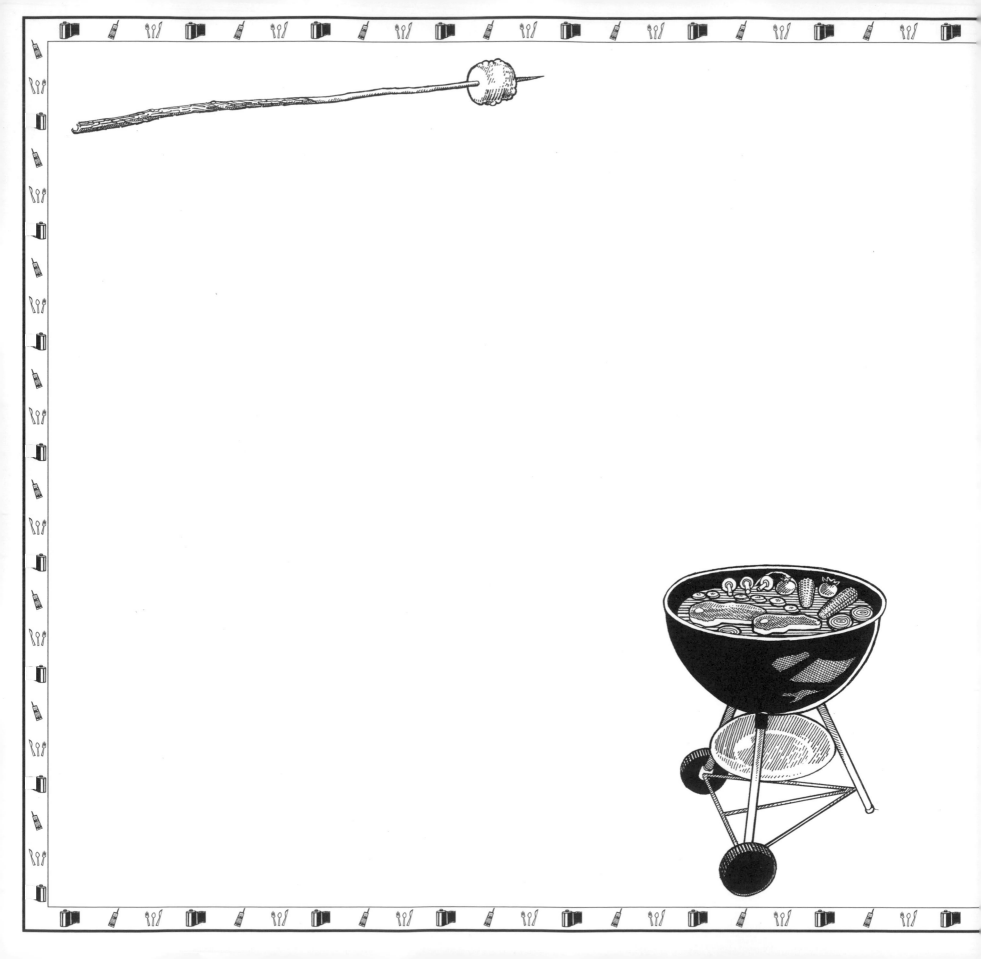

Unforgettable Feasts

Springtime in the Great Lakes begins an explosion of edible abundance—morel mushrooms, wild leeks, trout and whitefish, vegetables, cherries, berries, apples, pears . . . in a verdant setting of orchards, crystal lakes and a rainbow of wild flowers.

> – Harlan "Pete" Peterson, James Beard Foundation's Best Chef, Midwest nominee, and owner of the award-winning Tapawingo restaurant

Restaurants that rank supreme _____

_____

_____

_____

_____

Gourmet on the go _____

_____

_____

_____

_____

_____

Our creations! Venison and morels,
pan-fried brook trout, homegrown greens _____

_____

_____

_____

_____

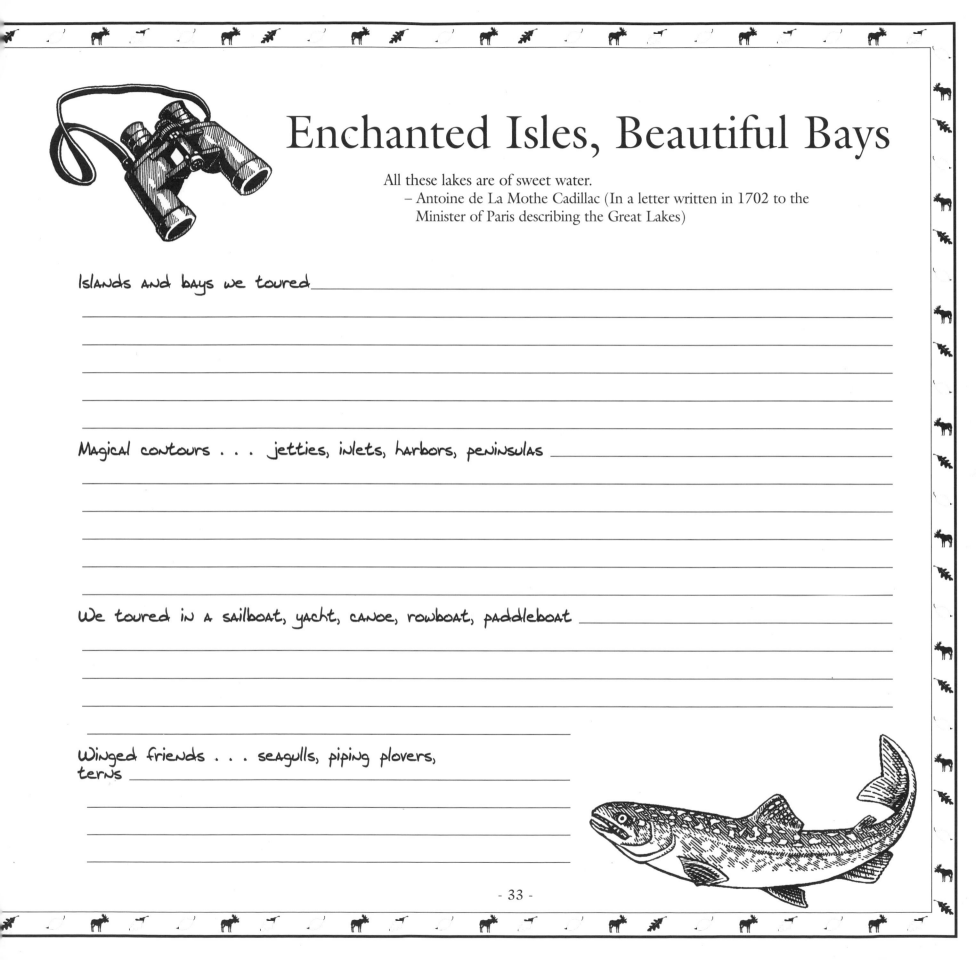

Enchanted Isles, Beautiful Bays

All these lakes are of sweet water.
– Antoine de La Mothe Cadillac (In a letter written in 1702 to the Minister of Paris describing the Great Lakes)

Islands and bays we toured _____
_____
_____
_____
_____

Magical contours . . . jetties, inlets, harbors, peninsulas _____
_____
_____
_____
_____

We toured in a sailboat, yacht, canoe, rowboat, paddleboat _____
_____
_____
_____
_____

Winged friends . . . seagulls, piping plovers,
terns _____
_____
_____
_____

At Play

... the greatest pleasure grounds in the world.
– James Oliver Curwood, *The Great Lakes*

Playtime! Golfing, water skiing, sailing, fishing, beach combing, swimming, biking _____

_____

_____

_____

_____

An adrenaline rush to remember _____

_____

_____

_____

_____

_____

_____

_____

Chilling out . . . . relaxing after a hard play's work _____

_____

_____

_____

_____

_____

Snafus

You don't watch for potholes around here, you watch for a little roadway between them.
– Raza Manji, quoted in *New York Times*, 14 July 1984

Waking up on the wrong side of the sleeping bag

Lasting lessons

Mishaps, forgotten keys, wrong turns, bad timing

On the Water

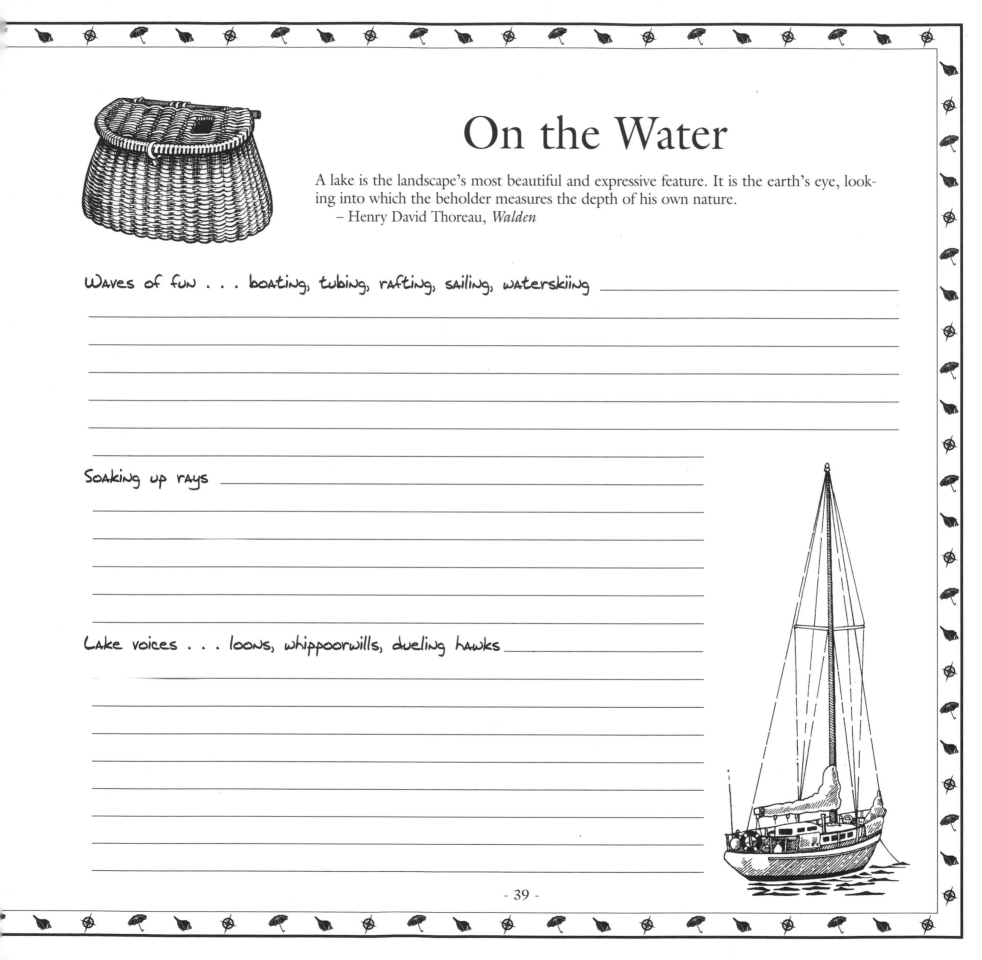

A lake is the landscape's most beautiful and expressive feature. It is the earth's eye, looking into which the beholder measures the depth of his own nature.
– Henry David Thoreau, *Walden*

Waves of fun . . . boating, tubing, rafting, sailing, waterskiing _____

_____

_____

_____

_____

_____

Soaking up rays _____

_____

_____

_____

_____

Lake voices . . . loons, whippoorwills, dueling hawks _____

_____

_____

_____

_____

_____

_____

Arts and Entertainment

Nature is a revelation of God; Art is a revelation of Man.
– Henry Wadsworth Longfellow

It's showtime! Plays, movies, concerts _____

_____

_____

_____

_____

_____

Artful excursions . . . galleries, museums, book-signings_____

_____

_____

_____

_____

Treasure hunting - sculptures, ceramics, photos,
antiques, folk art, quilts, rustic furniture _____

_____

_____

_____

_____

_____

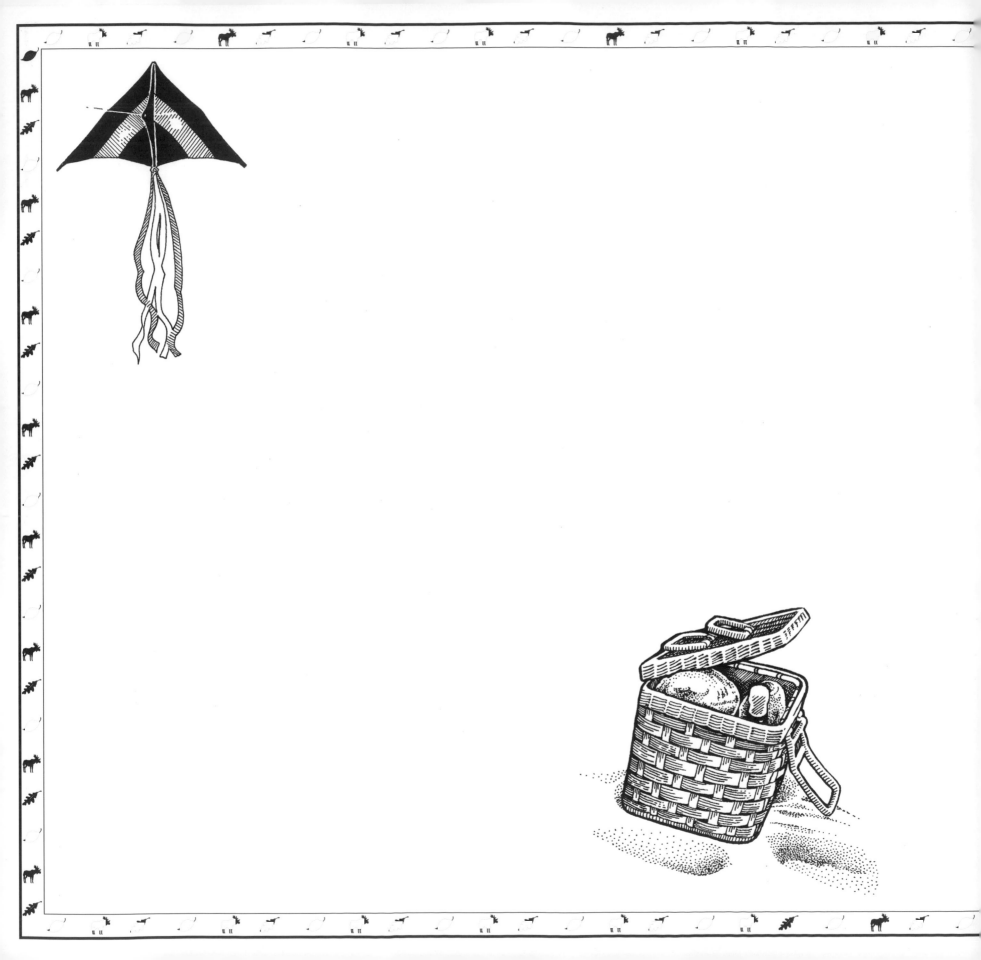

Sand Dunes

SAID THE
MOUNTAIN, I WILL
CHANGE SO SLOWLY THAT NO ONE
WILL NOTICE AND PEOPLE WILL FEEL
SECURE
SAID THE
SAND DUNE, I WILL
CHANGE WITH THE WIND SO
THAT ALL WILL SEE AND BE FILLED WITH
SURPRISE
 – Edna Elfont, *Sand Dunes of the Great Lakes*

Tripping to the top . . . dune climbs _____

_____

_____

_____

_____

Tumble-in-the-sand fun _____

_____

_____

_____

Dramatic dunescapes _____

_____

_____

Dune dwellers . . . mice, raccoons, birds _____

_____

_____

Celebrations

One joy scatters a hundred griefs.
– Chinese proverb

Summer fun! . . . amusement parks, parades, festivals, water slides _____

_____

_____

_____

_____

Delicious drinks, exquisite edibles, awesome bands _____

_____

_____

_____

_____

Merry-making on Main Street . . . . . fireworks, clowns, floats, elephant ears _____

_____

_____

The kids' highest five went to . . . _____

_____

_____

_____

_____

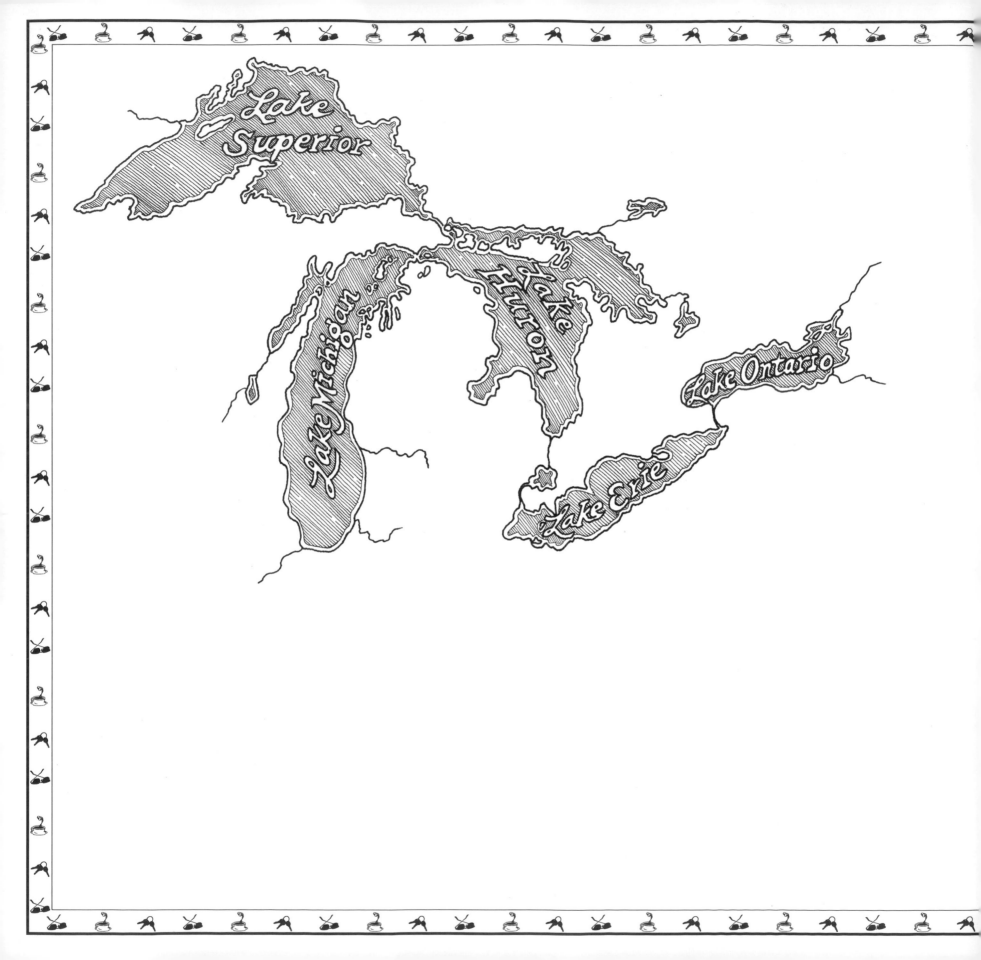

The Trail We Blazed

The end of all our exploring will be to arrive where we started and know the place for the first time.
 – T.S. Eliot

Tracking our trek . . . where we started, where we went, how we finished _____

_____

_____

_____

_____

_____

_____

_____

Lay of the land _____

_____

_____

_____

Picture perfect moments _____

_____

_____

_____

Lasting memories _____

_____

_____

_____

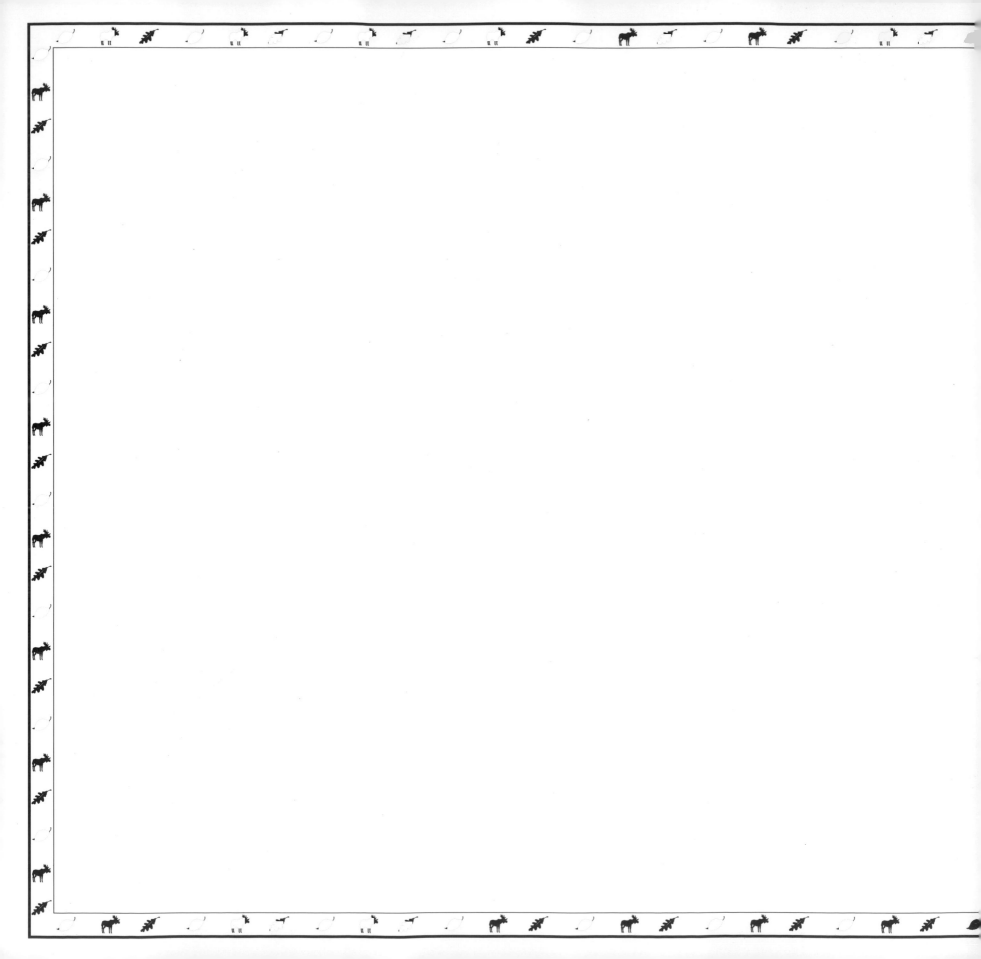

WIN A FOUR NIGHT STAY AT THE GRAND HOTEL ON MACKINAC ISLAND!

Enter Your Best Great Lakes Vacation Photo and Essay in the 1998 Great Lakes-Good Times Give-Away

OFFICIAL RULES

1. HOW TO ENTER

Ready, set...Get Creative! Just mail one copy of your favorite *Great Lakes Good Times* journal page, a reprint of one accompanying photo and the form below. If you are not purchasing the book, send in a 250-word essay, one photo and contact information on a 3x5 card (name, address, phone number, and date submitted). The essay/journal page and photo should vividly describe and portray your most treasured vacation memory, e.g., "Local Flavor", "Celebrations", "Snafus", etc..

Entries will be judged on creativity, photo quality, writing, and how well the essay relates to the photo. Please submit an actual reprint of your photo.

ENTRIES MUST BE SUBMITTED BY OCTOBER 1, 1998. WINNER WILL BE ANNOUNCED ON DECEMBER 1, 1998.

Mail your entry to:
Great Lakes Good Times Give-Away
135 E. 10th Street
Traverse City, MI 49684

ALL ENTRIES MUST INCLUDE:
Name, Address, Phone number and Date of entry.

2. GRAND PRIZE

WINNER GETS A GRAND VACATION! At the Grand Hotel, you can do it all...or nothing at all! Horse-drawn carriage tours, golf on the Jewel, tennis on clay courts, swimming in the magnificent serpentine pool. Horseback rides. Garden strolls. Shopping in a 19th century village. Bicycling. Picnics. Exploring the historic Fort Mackinac and the island forest pathways. Discover a whole new world of old-world charm and hospitality.

Your Four-Night Stay at the Four-Diamond Grand Hotel Will Include:

- One room, for up to four persons, between May 6 and October 31, 1999, subject to availability.

- Dinner on arrival day, breakfast and dinner on the second, third and fourth days, and breakfast on departure day for up to four persons.

- All taxes, tipping, and baggage handling charges as they pertain to the room and meals noted above.

3. GENERAL

Limit one entry per person. Multiple entries submitted by a single entrant are void. All entries become the property of Crystal River Press. Neither Crystal River Press nor its affiliates, subsidiaries, divisions, advertising, and promotion agencies are responsible for inaccurate transcription of entry information; any human error; technical, computer, telephone or telecommunications system malfunctions; lost or delayed data transmission; omissions; or any other error, malfunction, or late, lost, incomplete, deleted, or misdirected entries.

Prizes are not transferable and may not be substituted or exchanged except by sponsor due to unavailability. Prize winners will be required to execute an Affidavit of Eligibility/Liability and Publicity Release, which must be returned within fourteen (14) days of notification attempt; trip companions will be required to execute a Release of Liability prior to departure. Noncompliance may result in disqualification and award of prize to an alternate winner.

Odds of winning depend upon the number of eligible entries received. By participating entrants agree to be bound by these rules and the judges' decisions, and if selected as a winner, by accepting prize, agree to sponsor's use (unless prohibited by law) of his or her name, city of residence, photograph, and/or likeness for advertising and/or trade purposes without further permission or compensation. Winners will be notified by U.S. mail. Sponsor is not responsible for any virus, bugs, unauthorized human intervention, or other causes beyond the control of the sponsor that corrupt or affect the administration, security, fairness, or proper play or conduct of the giveaway.

By accepting prize, winners release Crystal River Press, Grand Hotel, and their parent companies, subsidiaries, affiliates, divisions, advertising , promotion, and production agencies from any and all liability for any loss, harm, damages, costs, or expenses, including without limitation property damages, personal injury, and/or death, arising out of participation in this giveaway or the acceptance, use or misuse of any prize. All federal, state, and local taxes are the sole responsibility of the winners. Any prize won by a minor will be awarded to the minor's parent or legal guardian.

NO PURCHASE NECESSARY TO PLAY OR RECEIVE A PRIZE.

4. ELIGIBILITY

The giveaway is open to legal residents of the United States. It is void in the state of Florida, Puerto Rico, the Virgin Islands, Guam, and wherever prohibited or restricted by applicable federal and state laws and regulations. Employees of Crystal River Press, Grand Hotel, and their parent companies, divisions, subsidiaries, affiliates, advertising, public relations, production, and promotion agencies and members of their immediate families (spouses, parents, children, and siblings and their spouses) are not eligible.